The Simple Life Cookbook

Recipes & notions that leave time for life's more important things

Erin Allred

The American Pantry Collection™

Published by:
Apricot Press
Box 98
Nephi, Utah
84648

books@apricotpress.com
www.apricotpress.com

Copyright 2004 by E. W. Allred
Second Edition

ISBN 1-885027-30-3

Cover Design & Layout by David Mecham
Printed in the United States of America

Forward

I had such a great time writing this book. It was a wonderful experience, and somewhat of a relief, to finally compile all the fast and easy recipes I love. I hoped this would be a book that many people would use on a regular basis. The book has also inspired me to organize my life a little better by using some of the time-saving tips I collected. I hope this book inspires you as well – we could all use a little more time in our day!

My Mom introduced me to the world of fast and easy cooking. She is an excellent cook, and also the queen of putting together a great meal in no time at all. I remember showing up after school with four or five of my friends and asking if they could stay for dinner. Amazingly, there was always a delicious meal and enough for everyone. Now, my husband and I stop by for dinner unannounced all the time (that's the great thing about living a block away from your parents!) and Mom somehow always has a great meal ready in seconds and what's even more amazing is that my 6-foot 4-inch husband is always full afterwards. Watching Mom, I realized that quick and easy cooking was a talent that I desperately needed to learn.

It all started when I went away to college. (I suspect that many people start cooking in college because Mom isn't around to cook for them!) One day I was in my dorm room making yet another batch of Top Ramen Noodles, and it hit me, if I ate another bite of "food from a box" I was going to puke. On top of that, I'd gained a few extra pounds. Who knew there were so many calories in one little box of Macaroni and Cheese! Unfortunately, I also knew that I didn't have a lot of time to prepare my meals. Sound familiar? After that, I started experimenting with my meals. It was a little scary at first, but I figured a few things out, mostly the hard way, and by asking my friends for advice. Soon I was cooking up a storm and even fixed some things that impressed the boys who came over begging for free food.

I later married and thought that my simple and easy cooking days were over. I knew I could make easy meals that I liked, but my husband was used to amazing home cooked meals. I envisioned myself spending hours over a hot stove fixing gourmet meals for my new family. Yeah, right! I soon realized that between work and school I didn't have the time and my poor husband was reduced to eating frozen burritos. Finally, after he refused to eat another bean and cheese chimichanga, I started to experiment with fast and easy meals again and realized that the skills I had learned would probably be useful to many people. I want everyone to know that there is an easier way to cook. No one has to know that dinner only took you 20 minutes. I sure won't tell. Try it out. You'll impress everyone you cook for, including yourself, and still have time left in your day for what's really important.

- Erin Allred

Recipes

When you only have 2 minutes...

If you just need a quick meal...

If you have to pack a lunch...

So easy kids can make them...

When you only have 2 minutes (Ok... maybe 10)

These recipes include meals that are prepackaged to cut the preparation and cooking time in half. All you need to do is mix in a few of your own ingredients and, violla, it looks like you made a meal from scratch and everyone will rave about the taste, only you'll know the secret.

Minute Rice plus Cheese

Minute Rice
American Cheese

Prepare minute rice as usual, but when water boils stir in
one slice (3/4 ounce) of cheese for each serving of rice.
Cover and remove from heat and let stand for 10 minutes.

Tomato Tortellini

Frozen Tortellini
Spaghetti Sauce
Parmesan Cheese

Cook frozen tortellini according to package directions,
drain and stir into heated spaghetti sauce. Top with
Parmesan cheese.

Cacciatore Chicken Sandwiches

Frozen Chicken Patties
Onion Buns
Marinara Sauce
Parmesan Cheese

Cook frozen chicken patties and toast onion buns. Place patties on buns, and top with heated marinara sauce and shredded Parmesan cheese.

Making the simple complicated is commonplace; making the complicated simple, awesomely simple, that's creativity.
- Charles Mingus

Life is really simple, but we insist on making it complicated.
- Confucius

Maybe a person's time would be as well spent raising food as raising money to buy food.
- Frank A. Clark

Italian Shrimp and Broccoli

Diced Garlic
Canned Tomatoes with Herbs
Frozen Broccoli
Cooked and Peeled Shrimp
Cooked Rice or Pasta

Heat diced garlic and herb tomatoes with frozen broccoli.
Stir in cooked shrimp and serve over rice or cooked pasta.

Creamy Chicken and Asparagus

Cooked Fresh Asparagus
Alfredo Sauce
Cooked and Diced Chicken
Cooked and Peeled Shrimp
Cooked Rice or Pasta

Cook fresh asparagus and add to bottled Alfredo sauce and
frozen cooked, diced chicken. Heat over low heat until
hot and serve over cooked fettuccine.

Swedish Meatballs

Frozen Meatballs
Brown Gravy
Sour Cream
Nutmeg
Mashed Potatoes

Heat frozen cooked meatballs with a jar of brown gravy in heavy saucepan. Stir in some sour cream and a bit of nutmeg. Serve on mashed potatoes, prepared according to package instructions.

Steak Supper

Beef Steaks
Soy Sauce
Mashed Potatoes

Broil your favorite type of steak. Add 2 teaspoons soy sauce to frozen mushrooms in butter sauce and heat according to package directions. Top steaks with sauce and serve over mashed potatoes prepared according to package instructions.

Cheesy Tortellini

Frozen Broccoli
Refrigerated Tortellini
Four Cheese Alfredo Sauce

Cook refrigerated tortellini and frozen broccoli in the same pot until pasta is tender and broccoli is heated through. Add refrigerated four cheese Alfredo sauce and heat.

Meatball Sandwiches

Frozen Meatballs
Spaghetti Sauce
Hoagie Buns
Mozzarella Cheese

Heat frozen cooked meatballs with a jar of spaghetti sauce. Spoon onto toasted hoagie buns and top with mozzarella cheese slices. Broil about 1 minute to melt cheese.

Chicken a la King

Alfredo Sauce
Cooked and Diced Chicken
Frozen Baby Peas
Chopped Pimento

Heat bottled Alfredo sauce with frozen diced cooked chicken, frozen baby peas, and some bottled chopped pimento. Serve over biscuits.

Chicken Cacciatore

Refrigerated Fettuccini
Frozen Broccoli
Canned Chicken
Canned Italian Tomatoes

Cook fettuccine according to package directions, adding frozen broccoli florets during the last 4 minutes of cooking time. Drain well, return to pot, and add 1 can cooked chicken, drained, and 1 can Italian seasoned diced tomatoes. Heat well and serve.

Smoked Salmon Pizza

Boboli Pizza Crust
Cream Cheese
Pesto
Cold-smoked Salmon Strips
Havarti Cheese

Top a Boboli pizza crust with softened cream cheese, then spoon refrigerated pesto on top. Top with cold-smoked salmon strips and Havarti cheese. Bake as directed on crust package.

The greatest truths are the simplest, and so are the greatest men. (and women)
*   - J.C. Hare*

One cannot collect all the beautiful shells on the beach. One can collect only a few, and they are more beautiful if they are few.
*   - Anne Morrow Lindbergh*

To know you have enough is to be rich.
*   - Tao Te Ching*

Olive Pizza

Boboli Pizza Crust
Chopped Olives
Salsa
Colby Jack Cheese

Top a Boboli pizza crust with chopped olives, salsa, and shredded Colby Jack cheese. Bake as directed on crust package.

Tuna Alfredo

Bow Tie Pasta
Frozen Mixed Vegetables
Canned Tuna
Alfredo Sauce

Cook bow tie pasta with frozen mixed vegetables and drain well. Mix with canned, drained tuna and refrigerated Alfredo sauce and heat.

Salsa Wraps

Chicken Breast Piece
Salsa
Flour Tortillas
Lettuce
Tomatoes
Cheese
Sour Cream

Brown chicken breast pieces in olive oil in skillet and stir in some salsa. Layer on heated tortillas with lettuce, tomatoes, cheese and sour cream. Fold tortilla and serve.

Pasta with Cream Sauce

Pasta
Frozen Mixed Vegetables
Mushroom Soup
Parmesan Cheese

Cook and drain 12 ounce. of pasta, then cook and drain 1 cup of frozen vegetables. Heat 1 can of cream of mushroom soup. Mix everything together and serve with Parmesan cheese.

Time Saving tips for your everyday life

I know we all want to save time in the kitchen, but there are many more opportunities to save a little time throughout the day. Give a few of these a try and have time for that walk in the park you can never seem to take.

Write or type up a list of your bills and the due dates. Make copies each month and highlight as you pay them. Sometimes we don't receive bills and this will save money on late fees. If you don't receive a bill just send payment with a note and your account number. Plus you don't have to rack your brain trying to remember if you paid something or not.

Call ahead - Verify everything – does the store have the item in stock, has the Little League game been cancelled, etc.

Group your errands and plan your route to save time, money and gas.

Don't wait in endless lines at the bank – use automatic deposit, automatic investing, online banking and auto-bill paying.

When you take something out, always return it to its place. Ten minutes a day looking for misplaced items wastes 60 hours a year.

Set aside 15 minutes each day to clean ONE area of your house. By the weekend, you won't have much more cleaning to do. Go have some fun!

Keep a lost-and-found section in a central location where family members can stash things they find lying around and look for things they have lost.

Never walk through the house empty-handed. Pick up and put away as you go.

Designate a drawer for healthful snacks like pretzels, rice cakes or trail mix, so the kids can help themselves when hungry.

Receiving guests with little notice? Gather toys, papers, shoes etc., in a laundry basket and put in a closet and close the door. Fluff pillow, close all doors, put dirty dishes in dishwasher, wipe countertops and quickly dust surfaces.

When loading the dishwasher, group knives, forks and spoons together to reduce sorting time.

Spray cloth place mats and seat covers with a fabric protector to remove any spills or stains with ease.

Keep takeout menus at work so you can order dinner to pick up on the way home when you are really running behind.

Designate a file for each child. Tell your kids to place any material you need to review in it as soon as they get home from school.

Keep a cooler in the trunk of your car. You can stop for groceries anytime without having to go straight home.

Call ahead to find out if the doctor is running late to find out what time you should really come in.

Once a week, prepackage chips, cookies, nuts, dried fruits, raisins and other goodies in plastic sandwich bags and store them in a large sealed container. When it's time to fix your family's lunch, toss the prepared bags into the lunch box or sack, along with a sandwich and fruit. This really saves time in the morning.

When you just need a quick meal, but nothing too fancy

These recipes are perfect if you need something quick for your family or friends or even just yourself. They are some of my favorites, most of which I grew up on. So enjoy; they're sure to become some of your favorites as well.

Quick & Easy Chicken Enchiladas

Prep time: 30 minutes
Cooking time: 20 minutes

> 2 cups cooked, shredded, boneless, skinless
>   chicken breast meat
> 2 (10-ounce) cans enchilada sauce
> 1 cup Mexican blend or Monterey jack cheese
> 1 (4-ounce) can diced green chilies
> 8 (6-inch) corn tortillas

1. Preheat oven to 350° F. Grease 11x7 inch baking dish
2. Spread 1/2 cup enchilada sauce onto bottom of prepared baking dish. Combine chicken, 1/2 cup enchilada sauce, 1/2 cup cheese and chilies in medium bowl.
3. Spoon chicken mixture evenly down center of each tortilla, roll up.
4. Place seam-side down in baking dish. Top with remaining enchilada sauce and cheese.
5. Bake for 15 to 20 minutes or until heated through and cheese is melted

Chicken & Rice Bake

Prep time: 15 minutes
Cooking time: 2 hours

    1-1/2 cups uncooked rice
    12-14 chicken breast strips
    Salt to taste
    1 can cream of mushroom soup
    2 chicken bouillon cubes
    3 cups boiling water

1. Spread uncooked rice in large dripping pan
2. Lay chicken in the rice
3. Salt to taste, cover with 1 can cream of mushroom soup
4. Dissolve 2 chicken bouillon cubes in 3 cups boiling water and pour carefully around corners of pan.
5. Bake 1 hour, uncovered, at 350° F
6. Cover and bake one hour longer.

Easy Chuck Steak

Prep time: 5 minutes
Cook time: 45 minutes

    1 or 2 chuck steaks
    1 package dry onion soup mix
    2 small cans mushrooms steams and pieces

1. Preheat oven to 350° F.
2. Line a shallow baking pan with enough aluminum foil to seal, place chuck steaks in pan.
3. Sprinkle onion soup mix over meat and then add the mushrooms (liquid too).
4. Seal the foil and bake for 45 minutes.

Beware the barrenness of a busy life.
*   - Socrates*

Little drops of water, little grains of sand, make the mighty ocean and the pleasant land. So the little minutes, humble though they be, make the mighty ages of eternity.
*   - Julia A. Fletcher*

Chicken Pot Pie

Prep time: 5 minutes
Cook time: 35 to 40 minutes

1 bag frozen mixed veggies
1 can soup, either cream of mushroom, cream of
    celery, or cheddar cheese
1/2 to 1 onion
1 can of chicken breast pieces or 1 box frozen
    chicken cubes
2 ready-to-bake frozen pie crusts

1. Preheat oven to 375° F.
2. Thaw chicken in microwave according to directions if using frozen.
3. Dice onion.
4. In medium size mixing bowl stir in mixed veggies, soup, onion, and chicken together.
5. Pour mixture into one of the crusts. Turn the other crust pan upside down so that the crust inside it forms a top for the pie. Remove the top pan and press the edges of the pie pastry to the lower crust and pan.
6. Bake for 35 to 40 minutes.

Homemade Chicken Fingers

2 cups Cap'n Crunch cereal
1-1/2 cups corn flakes
1 large egg
1 cup milk
1 cup flour
1 teaspoon onion powder
1 teaspoon garlic powder
1/2 teaspoon pepper
Vegetable oil for frying
2 pounds boneless, skinless chicken breast,
    cut into 1-ounce pieces

1. Coarsely crush both the cereals with a rolling pin, set aside.
2. In a bowl, beat 1 egg with 1 cup milk until combined.
3. In a shallow bowl, stir together the flour, onion and garlic powders and pepper.
4. In a large skillet, heat 1-inch vegetable oil over medium-high heat until hot but not smoking, 325° F. on a deep-fat thermometer. As the oil heats, prepare the chicken: Dip the pieces, 1 at a time, into the seasoned flour, then into the egg mixture, then into the cereal, coating on all sides. Place the chicken pieces carefully in the hot oil and cook until golden brown and cooked through about 3 to 5

minutes, depending on the size of the pieces.
5. Transfer the chicken pieces to a paper towels to drain
and cool slightly.

The good and the wise lead quiet lives.
- Euripides

*Dealing with complexity is an inefficient and
unnecessary waste of time, attention and mental energy.
There is never any justification for things being complex
when they could be simple.*
- Edward de Bono

There is more to life than increasing its speed.
- Mohandas K. Gandhi

Potato Burrito

Prep time: 15 minutes

    1 (16-ounce) package frozen hash brown potatoes
    1 cup chunky salsa
    2 cups shredded cheddar cheese
    1/4 cup green onion
    6 flour tortillas

1. Cook hash brown potatoes as directed on package.
2. Add salsa, cheese and green onion
3. Fold mixture into warmed flour tortillas and serve.

An expert is someone who has succeeded in making decisions and judgments simpler through knowing what to pay attention to and what to ignore.
        - Edward de Bono

To simplify complications is the first essential of success.
        - George Earle Buckle

When the solution is simple, God is answering.
        - Albert Einstein

Taco Salad

Prep time: 20 minutes

1 onion
2 tomatoes
1 head of lettuce
1 cup grated cheese
1 pound ground beef
1 can kidney beans
Diced avocado
1 bag Doritos chips
Salt and pepper

1. Brown ground beef and drain off fat, add salt and pepper to taste.
2. Chop onion, tomatoes and lettuce and toss with cheese.
3. Add beans to ground beef.
4. Chop up avocado.
5. Prepare dressing – Thousand Island
6. Add salsa to taste.
7. Serve all over chips.

Hamburger Pizza

Prep time: 30 minutes

1 can (28-ounce) whole Italian tomatoes, drained
1 pound ground chuck
1 1/2 teaspoons salt
1 teaspoon prepared mustard, or to taste
1 teaspoon Worcestershire sauce, or to taste
1/2 teaspoon ground black pepper
1/4 teaspoon prepared horseradish, or to taste
2 tablespoons chopped onion
2 tablespoons chopped parsley
1-1/2 teaspoons chopped fresh oregano or
    1/2 teaspoon dried
1 teaspoon chopped fresh basil or
    1/4 teaspoon dried
1 cup packaged combined shredded mozzarella
    and grated Parmesan and Romano cheeses

1. Slice each tomato in half and drain in a colander.
2. In a bowl, combine the ground chuck, salt, mustard, Worcestershire, pepper, and horseradish. Press the beef mixture into a 10-inch pie plate as if you were pressing in a piecrust.
3. Top the beef mixture with the tomatoes. Sprinkle the

onion, parsley, oregano, and basil on top of the tomatoes.
Sprinkle cheese on top.
4. After baking, wait 15 minutes before slicing. If there is
any liquid in the pie plate, drain before serving.

*Slow down and enjoy life. It's not only the scenery you
miss by going to fast, you also miss the sense of where
you are going and why.*
　　　　　　　- Eddie Cantor

*The ability to simplify means to eliminate the
unnecessary so that the necessary may speak.*
　　　　　　　- Hans Hofmann

*A little simplification would be the first step toward
rational living, I think.*
　　　　　　　- Eleanor Roosevelt

Summer Squash Casserole

Prep time: 25 minutes
Cooking time: 30 minutes

    7 cups vegetables (zucchini, summer squash,
        carrots, etc.)
    1 cup sour cream
    1 can cream of chicken soup
    Stove Top stuffing

1. Dice vegetables and boil until tender, drain off liquid.
2. Mix together sour cream and chicken soup and add to vegetable mixture. Put in 9x13 pan.
3. Make Stove Top stuffing mix and spread on top.
4. Bake for 30 minutes at 350° F.

We learn from our gardens to deal with the most urgent question of the time: How much is enough?
                            - Wendell Berry

Microwave Scrambled Eggs

Prep time: 10 minutes

1/4 cup butter
8 eggs, beaten
1/4 cup milk
1/4 cup Parmesan cheese
1/2 tsp. Salt
1/4 teaspoon white pepper

1. Place butter in a large microwave safe bowl. Microwave on high until butter melts, about 60-90 seconds.
2. Mix eggs, milk, Parmesan cheese, salt, and pepper in another large bowl and beat well.
3. Pour into hot butter. Microwave on high until eggs are set but still slightly moist, about 2-3 minutes.
4. Remove from microwave and cover; let stand on solid surface until eggs become firm, about 2-3 minutes.
5. Return to microwave for 30-second intervals if eggs aren't done to your liking.

Turkey & Rice Casserole

1 can cream of chicken soup
1 can cream of mushroom soup
3/4 cup water
2 cups turkey
1/2 cup rice

Mix and bake at 325° F for 1 hour and 15 minutes.

The trouble with so many of us is that we underestimate the power of simplicity. We have a tendency it seems to over complicate our lives and forget what's important and what's not. We tend to mistake movement for achievement. We tend to focus on activities instead of results. And as the pace of life continues to race along in the outside world, we forget that we have the power to control our lives regardless of what's going on outside.
- Robert Stuberg

Simplicity is making the journey of this life with just baggage enough.
- Anonymous

Broccoli & Rice Casserole

Prep time: 20 minutes
Cooking time: 35 minutes

1/2 cup chopped onion
1 can cream of chicken soup
1 cup minute rice
1 small jar Cheese Whiz
4 tablespoons butter
1 cup milk
2 packages (10-ounce) frozen chopped broccoli

1. Sauté onion in butter. Add soup, milk and rice.
2. Cook broccoli, drain, combine with cheese.
3. Add to rice, mix.
4. Bake 350° F for 35 minutes.

Stuffed Baked Potatoes

Prep time: 15 minutes
Cooking time: 20 minutes

    6 baking potatoes
    1 cup sour cream
    1/2 cup butter, softened
    1 package (3-ounce) cream cheese
    1 teaspoon salt
    1 teaspoon pepper
    3/4 cup grated cheddar cheese

1. Bake potatoes. Let cool (it's a good idea to bake them the day before).
2. Cut in half lengthwise. Spoon potato into bowl, set shells aside.
3. To potato add sour cream, butter, cream cheese, onions, salt, pepper, whip until light.
4. Add milk only if necessary, fold in cheese.
5. Fill shells.
6. Put on cookie sheet, bake at 350° F for 20 minutes.

Broccoli & Pasta

Prep time: 20 minutes

    1/4 cup olive oil
    2-1/2 cups fresh broccoli florets
    3 large cloves garlic
    1/4 teaspoon crushed red pepper
    1 package (9-ounce) refrigerated Fettuccine
    1/3 cup shredded Romano Cheese

1. Heat oil in large skillet; add broccoli, garlic and crushed red pepper.
2. Cook, stirring frequently, until broccoli is crisp-tender.
3. Add pasta. Toss to coat well. Sprinkle with cheese and toss lightly. Serve immediately.

Remember that in giving any reason at all for refusing, you lay some foundation for a future request.
- Arthur Helps

You have succeeded in life when all you really want is only what you really need.
- Vernon Howard

Chicken Casserole

Prep time: 30 minutes
Cook time: 20 minutes

    3 medium chicken breasts (boneless & skinless)
    4 cups bread crumbs
    1 can cream of chicken soup
    1 can cream of celery soup
    2 cans mixed vegetables, drained
    Salt and pepper

1. Boil chicken breasts until completely cooked.
2. In separate bowl mix both cans of soup, 1/2 of the breadcrumbs, and both cans of mixed vegetables. Add salt and pepper to this mixture.
3. Mix soup mixture and chicken into casserole pan, sprinkle remaining bread crumbs on top of casserole.
4. Heat oven to 350° F. Bake casserole until all contents are thoroughly heated.

Easy Meat Loaf

Prep time: 5 minutes
Cooking time: 1 hour

   2 pounds ground beef
   1 package Lipton onion soup mix
   1 can evaporated milk
   1 cup ketchup

1. Mix hamburger, soup mix, and evaporated milk into a large bowl, mix completely and form a loaf.
2. Place into loaf pan and cook in pre heated oven (325°) for 1 hour, draining off any excess grease every 15 minutes.
3. About 15 minutes before the loaf has finished cooking, add ketchup to top and finish baking.

Frugality is one of the most beautiful and joyful words in the English language, and yet one that we are culturally cut off from understanding and enjoying. The consumption society has made us feel that happiness lies in having things, and has failed to teach us the happiness of not having things.
                                 - Elise Boulding

Southwestern Pita Pockets

Prep time: 5 minutes

    1 cup mild salsa
    1/2 cup mayonnaise
    6 pitas
    12 slices smoked turkey or chicken
    12 slices Pepper Jack cheese
    2 cups shredded lettuce
    1 cup sliced ripe black olives

1. Combine half the salsa and mayonnaise in a small bowl.
2. In each pita half, place a slice of turkey, a slice of cheese, lettuce and olives. Top with remaining salsa.

The art of contentment is the recognition that the most satisfying and most dependably refreshing experiences of life lie not in great things but in little. The rarity of happiness among those who achieved much is evidence that achievement is not in itself the assurance of a happy life. The great, like the humble, may have to find their satisfaction in the same plain things.
- Edgar A. Collard

Cheesy Corn Dip

Prep time: 5 minutes

    8-ounces sour cream
3/4 cup mayonnaise
3/4 teaspoon ground cumin
3 (11-ounce) can mexicorn
2-1/2 cups shredded cheddar cheese
1 (7-ounce) can diced green chilies
2/3 cup sliced green onions

1. Combine sour cream, mayonnaise and cumin in medium bowl. Stir in mexicorn, cheese, green chilies and onions.
2. Serve with tortilla chips

With a few flowers in my garden, half a dozen pictures and some books, I live without envy.
- Lope de Vega

Chili Relleno Casserole

Prep time: 10 minutes
Cooking time: 1 hour

    1 (4-ounce) can green chilies, chopped
    1/2 pound Cheddar cheese, grated
    1/2 pound Jack cheese, grated
    1 can evaporated milk
    2 eggs, beaten

1. Layer an oblong baking dish with 2/3 of the Jack cheese and 2/3 of the Cheddar cheese.
2. Mix chilies, eggs, and milk, pour over cheese. Top with remaining cheese.
3. Bake for 1 hour at 350° F or until brown on top.

We don't need to increase our goods nearly as much as we need to scale down our wants. Not wanting something is as good as possessing it.
                                        - Donald Horban

Rice Casserole

Prep time: 15 minutes
Cooking time: 1 hour

1 cup rice
1 onion, copped
2 cans chicken broth
Fresh mushrooms
1 stick of butter

1. Put 1 cup rice in casserole dish.
2. Sauté fresh mushrooms and onion in 1 stick of butter.
3. Pour 2 cans of chicken broth over rice. Then pour sautéed mushrooms and onion over rice, stir and add pepper to taste.
4. Cook uncovered for 1 hour at 350° F.

The sculptor produces the beautiful statue by chipping away such parts of the marble block as are not needed. It is a process of elimination.
                    - Elbert Hubbard

Sloppy Jo's

Prep time: 25 minutes

    1/2 pound ground beef
    1 can Campbell's veggie beef soup
    2 tablespoons catsup
    1/2 teaspoon mustard
    1 teaspoon Worcestershire sauce

1. Brown ground beef and drain off fat.
2. Add veggie beef soup, catsup, mustard, Worcestershire sauce and mix.
3. Rinse soup can and add 1/3 can water to above mixture.
4. Simmer on low heat 10-15 minutes or until thickened to desired consistency.
5. Spoon onto hamburger bun.

Most of the critical things in life, which become the starting points for human destiny, are little things.
- R. Smith

Luscious Potatoes

Prep time: 5 minutes
Cooking time: 1 hour

    1 (2-pound) package hashed brown potatoes
    2 cans cream of potato soup
    1 pint sour cream
    Salt and pepper to taste
    2 cups grated cheddar cheese

1. Combine all ingredients except cheese in large casserole; mix well.
2. Sprinkle with cheese. Bake in preheated 350° F oven for 1 hour.

Manifest plainness, embrace simplicity, reduce selfishness, and have few desires.
               - Lao-Tzu, Tao Te Ching

Breakfast Quesadilla

Prep time: 25 minutes

    1 or 2 Eggs
    1 slice cheese
    1 tortilla
    link sausage

1. Scramble the eggs.
2. Fry sausage for 2-4 minutes until browned in same pan.
3. Melt cheese on tortilla in microwave.
4. Chop sausage into pieces.
5. Combine and eat.

Enjoy the little things, for one day you may look back and realize they were the big things.
    - Robert Brault

Sweet & Sour Chicken Nuggets

Prep time: 20 minutes

  12-15 frozen chicken nuggets
  1/2 onion
  1 bell pepper
  1 large carrot
  1 stalk of celery
  1 (4-ounce) can pineapple
  1 package instant sweet and sour mix

1. Chop vegetables.
2. Cook chicken nuggets in the oven.
3. Stir-fry vegetables then add chicken nuggets and pineapple.
4. Add instant sweet and sour mixture and follow the directions on the package.

Microwave Mexican Cube Steaks

Prep time: 15 minutes

    4 beef cube steaks
    1 cup salsa
    1 cup shredded Monterey Jack cheese
    1 avocado, peeled and sliced

1. Arrange steaks in an 8" square microwave safe dish.
2. Cover loosely with waxed paper and cook on high for 6-8 minutes, turning beef over after 3 minutes, until almost done. Drain.
3. Top each steak with salsa. Cover loosely with waxed paper and cook on high for 2-3 minutes or until salsa is hot.
4. Sprinkle each with cheese and cover. Let stand 2 minutes until cheese is melted.
5. Top with avocado slices and serve.

Rigatoni with Sun-Dried Tomato Pesto

Prep time: 25 minutes

4 quarts water
Salt to taste
1 pound rigatoni
4 garlic cloves
1 jar (8-ounces) sun-dried tomatoes packed in
    olive oil
1/4 cup pine nuts
1/2 cup grated Parmesan cheese
Salt and freshly ground pepper

1. Cook the rigatoni: pour the water into a large pot, salt lightly, and cover. Bring to a boil over high heat. Add the rigatoni, stir to separate, and cook according to the directions on the package, until al dente. Drain in a colander and return to the pot. Keep warm, covered.
2. Make the pesto: Coarsely chop the garlic.
3. In a food processor, combine the sun-dried tomatoes, including the oil, the pine nuts, garlic, and Parmesan and process to a smooth paste, stopping to scrape down the sides of the bowl with a rubber spatula once or twice. Makes 1 1/2 cups.
4. Add 1/2 cup of the pesto, or more to taste, to the rigatoni and toss well to combine. Season with salt and pepper. Cover and keep warm.

Chicken Fried Steak

Prep time: 15 minutes

4 round steaks (1-1/4 to 1-1/2 pounds)
2 large eggs
1/4 cup milk
1-1/2 cups all-purpose flour
Salt and pepper to taste
Canola oil for frying

1. Pat the steaks dry with paper towels.
2. In a shallow bowl, beat the eggs together with the milk until combined.
3. Spread the flour out on a large plate. Dip 1 steak at a time into the egg mixture, letting the excess drip off, then into the flour, shaking off any excess. Place on a baking sheet and season on both sides with salt and pepper. Prepare the remaining 3 steaks in the same manner.
4. Heat a large heavy skillet, preferably cast iron, over medium-high heat until hot. Add 1/4 inch canola oil and heat until hot, almost smoking. Carefully add 2 steaks and fry for 2 minutes. Turn and fry for 2 minutes, or until golden brown and crisp. Transfer the steaks to a large platter and keep warm. Add more oil to the skillet, if necessary, and cook the remaining 2 steaks in the same manner.

Cream Gravy

Prep time: 20 minutes

1 tablespoon butter
1/2 cup chopped scallions
1 cup fat-free reduced-sodium chicken broth
1/2 cup half-&-half
2 tablespoons all-purpose flour
Salt to taste
Cayenne pepper to taste
Worcestershire sauce to taste

1. In the skillet in which you cooked the steaks, melt the butter over medium heat. Add the scallions and cook, stirring for 2 minutes.
2. In a bowl, stir together the broth, half-and-half, and flour until blended. Add to the skillet, and bring to a boil, stirring. Simmer, stirring occasionally, until thickened, about 2 minutes. Add salt, cayenne, and Worcestershire sauce to taste.
3. Put 1 steak on each dinner plate, spoon cream gravy over it.

Asian Pork and Noodles

Prep time: 45 minutes

    2 cups water
    1 can (14-ounce) lite coconut milk
    3 teaspoons Thai yellow curry paste (or powder)
    2 packages (3-ounce) chicken-flavored ramen
        noodle soup
    1 large red pepper
    2 cups unsalted peanuts
    1 tablespoon vegetable oil
    1 pound pork for stir-fry
    1 cup chopped scallions
    Lime wedges

1. Pour the water into a large pot or Dutch oven, cover, and bring to a boil over high heat. Add the coconut milk, 2 teaspoons of yellow curry paste, and the seasoning packets from the soup mixes. Stir – reduce the heat slightly, and boil for 3 minutes. Add the noodles and cook, stirring frequently, for 2 minutes, or until the noodles soften. Cover and remove the pan from the heat.
2. Thinly slice the red pepper. Chop the peanuts and reserve.
3. In a large nonstick skillet, heat the vegetable oil and remaining 1 teaspoon curry paste over high heat, stirring to blend. Add the pork and stir-fry for 1 minute. Add the

pepper slices and stir-fry for 2 to 3 minutes, until the pork is cooked through and the peppers are slightly tender. Stir in the scallions.

4. Divide the noodles and sauce among 4 soup or pasta bowls. Top with the pork stir-fry. Sprinkle chopped peanuts over each bowl, garnish each with a lime wedge, if desired, and serve.

Two wings lift a person up from earthly concerns: simplicity in intention, and purity in feeling.
- Thomas Kempis

You can't have everything; where would you put it?
- Steven Wright

Teach us delight in the simple things, and mirth that has no bitter springs; Forgiveness free of evil done, and love to all men beneath the sun.
- Rudyard Kipling

Angel Hair Pasta & Chicken with Oriental Dressing

Prep time: 30 minutes

> 1 (9-ounce) package Angel hair pasta
> 1/3 cup creamy peanut butter
> 1/3 cup dark sesame oil
> 1/3 cup vegetable oil
> 1/4 cup orange juice
> 3 tablespoons rice vinegar
> 2 tablespoon Soy Sauce
> 1 tablespoon honey mustard
> 2 teaspoons hot chili oil
> 1-1/2 cups diced cooked chicken
> 1/3 cup sliced green onion

1. Prepare pasta according to directions, drain, and cool.
2. Combine peanut butter, sesame oil, vegetable oil, orange juice, vinegar, soy sauce, mustard and chili oil in small bowl. Mix until smooth. Season with salt and ground black pepper.
3. Toss pasta, chicken, green onions and dressing in medium bowl.

Fettuccine Tomato Basil Salad

Prep time: 25 minutes

1 (9-ounce) package Fettuccine
1 tablespoon olive oil
1 tablespoon red wine vinegar
1/4 cup grated Parmesan cheese
1/4 cup chopped fresh basil
1 pound fresh tomatoes

1. Prepare pasta according to package directions.
2. Toss pasta with oil, vinegar and cheese; add basil and tomatoes.
3. Season with salt and ground pepper.

The ordinary arts we practice every day at home are of more importance to the soul than their simplicity might suggest.
    - Thomas More

For peace of mind, we need to resign as general manager of the universe.
    - Larry Eisenberg

Fettuccine Alfredo

Prep time: 25 minutes

4 quarts water
Salt to taste
12 ounces fettuccine, fresh or dried
1 cup evaporated skimmed milk
1/2 cup nonfat sour cream
1 cup grated Parmesan cheese, plus additional
    for serving
2 tablespoons butter
Freshly ground pepper to taste

1. Cook the pasta. Pour the water into a large pot, salt lightly, and cover. Bring to a boil over high heat. Add the fettuccine, stir to separate the strands, and cook according to the directions on the package until just al dente. Drain well in a colander and return to the pot.
2. In a medium saucepan, heat the evaporated skimmed milk until hot. Remove the pan from the heat and stir in the sour cream and the Parmesan until thoroughly combined. Add the butter, place the pan over low heat, and cook, stirring, until the butter is melted and the sauce has thickened slightly.
3. Pour the sauce over the pasta, toss to coat the strands, then add a generous amount of fresh black pepper to taste. Toss to combine.

Chicken Parmesan

Prep time: 35 minutes

4 skinless and boneless chicken breast halves
Salt and pepper
1/2 teaspoon oregano
4 slices mozzarella
1-1/2 cups spaghetti sauce
1/4 cup grated Parmesan cheese

1. Lay the chicken in a baking pan and season with salt pepper, and oregano.
2. Cover the chicken with the mozzarella slices, pour the spaghetti sauce over the cheese, sprinkle with parmesan, cover loosely with foil and bake in a 350° F oven for about 25 minutes or until the chicken is cooked through.
3. Remove the cover and slide under the broiler to brown the top.

Simplicity involves unburdening your life, and living more lightly with fewer distractions that interfere with a high quality life, as defined uniquely by each individual. You will find people living simply in large cities, rural areas and everything in between.
                                    - Linda Breen Pierce

Tortilla Casserole

Prep time: 45 minutes

2 cups shredded cooked chicken
10 corn tortillas (6-inch diameter)
1 cup fat-free reduced-sodium chicken broth
2 tablespoons all-purpose flour
1/2 teaspoon ground cumin
1 package (10-ounces) frozen Southwestern-style
    corn and roasted red peppers, thawed
1 jar (11-1/2 to 12-ounces) salsa
1 cup shredded Mexican cheese mixture

1. Preheat the broiler if you are going to brown the top of the casserole. Grease a shallow 2-quart microwave-safe baking dish.

2. Shred the chicken, if necessary. Cut the stack of tortillas into quarters.

3. In a 1-quart saucepan, whisk together the broth, flour, and cuminutes Cover and bring to a boil over medium-heat. Cook, stirring, until the sauce has thickened. Stir in the chicken.

4. Assemble the casserole: In the prepared baking dish, layer 1/3 of the tortilla pieces. Top with the corn and peppers with any sauce, 1/2 of the remaining tortilla pieces, the chicken mixture, the remaining tortilla pieces, salsa,

and, finally, the cheese. Cover loosely with a piece of waxed paper, making sure that it does not touch the cheese. Microwave on high 8 to 10 minutes, or until the center of the casserole is hot.

5. If you want to brown the cheese on top, remove the piece of waxed paper and run the dish under the broiler for 1 to 2 minutes, until the cheese is lightly browned.

Baked Steak

Prep time: 2 minutes
Cooking time: 2-1/2 hours

> 2 pounds round steak
> 1 can cream of mushroom soup
> 1 package dry onion soup mix

1. Place round steak on large piece of heavy aluminum foil. Pour cream of mushroom soup on half the steak; sprinkle onion soup mix on soup.

2. Fold the other half of steak over this. Wrap foil securely. Place in open baking dish.

3. Bake at 350° F for 2 hours to 2 1/2 hours.

Microwave Red Snapper Veracruz

Prep time: 15 minutes

2 pound Fresh or frozen red snapper fillets, skinned
1 tomato, chopped
1/2 cup onion, chopped
1/2 cup green pepper, chopped
4 tablespoons butter or margarine
2 tablespoons lemon juice
1 clove garlic, minced
1/4 pound Fresh mushrooms, sliced or 1 can sliced
    mushrooms, drained
3 tablespoons chili sauce
1/4 teaspoon salt
Several dashes Tabasco sauce
1 can small shrimp
1/4 cup dry white wine

1. Thaw fish if frozen.
2. In glass baking dish, combine all ingredients, except fish, shrimp and wine. Cover with wax paper. Microwave on maximum power for 5 to 6 minutes or until vegetables are tender.
3. Stir in shrimp and wine.
4. Place fish fillets atop, spoon some of sauce over.
5. Microwave covered for 4 minutes more or until fish flakes when tested with a fork.

To simplify complications is the first essential of success.
        - George Earle Buckle

He lacks much who has no aptitude for idleness.
        - Louise Beebe Wilder

Go confidently in the direction of your dreams! Live the life you've imagined. As you simplify your life, the laws of the universe will be simpler; solitude will not be solitude, poverty will not be poverty, nor weakness.
        - Henry David Thoreau

Meat Balls

Prep time: 5 minutes
Cooking time: 1 hour & 30 minutes

1 pound ground beef
1/2 cup uncooked rice
1/2 teaspoon salt
1/4 teaspoon pepper
2 tablespoons chopped onion
1 can tomato soup

1. Mix thoroughly all ingredients except tomato soup.
2. Form into 12 balls. Place in greased casserole dish.
3. Pour soup over meat.
4. Bake, covered, in a 350° F for 1 hour and 30 minutes.

Being rich is having money, being wealthy is having time.
- Stephen Swid

The secret of your future is hidden in your daily routine.
- Mike Murdock

Mushroom Spinach Wraps

Prep time: 30 minutes

4 cups mushrooms, sliced
8 cups fresh spinach, rinsed, stemmed and
   coarsely chopped
4 9-in wraps or flour tortillas
1 cup shredded cheddar cheese
Salsa

1. Preheat oven to 400° F.
2. In large skillet, cook mushrooms with 2 tablespoons water over medium heat, covered, until tender, about 9 minutes.
3. Add spinach, cover and cook just until wilted, about 4 minutes. Drain well.
4. Divide mushroom-spinach mixture among wraps, spooning down center of each. Sprinkle with cheese and some salsa if desired.
5. Wrap up snugly and place on a baking sheet. Bake just until heated through, about 5 minutes. Serve.

Microwave Shrimp Scampi

Prep time: 20 minutes

1/2 cup butter
5 cloves garlic, minced
2 tablespoons lemon juice
2 tablespoons dried parsley flakes
1/2 teaspoon salt
1/4 teaspoon pepper
1 pound medium shrimp, peeled and deveined

1. In a shallow microwave-baking dish, combine all ingredients except shrimp.
2. Cook, uncovered on high power for 3-4 minutes or until butter is melted and mixture is hot stirring once during cooking.
3. Add shrimp and stir to coat. Cover with microwave safe plastic wrap, venting one corner, on high for 3-5 minutes or until shrimp curl and turn pink.
4. Let stand on solid surface, covered, for 3-5 minutes before serving.

If you want to make good use of your time, you've got to know what's most important and then give it all you've got.
-Lee Lacocca

Chicken Roll-Ups

Prep time: 35 minutes   Cooking time: 20 minutes

   8 ounces chicken breast
   8 ounces cream cheese
   5 tablespoons butter
   1 4-ounce can mushrooms (optional)
   3 cans crescent rolls
   2/3 cup breadcrumbs
   1/2 teaspoon poultry seasoning
   1/2 cup chopped nuts

1. Boil chicken in salt water, cook and remove meat from pot, let cool. Save broth.
2. Make filling: beat cream cheese and butter until smooth.
3. Fold in mushrooms.
4. Spread filling on a crescent roll and add chicken. Roll up and make sure chicken is covered by roll.
5. Make crumb mixture: mix breadcrumbs, poultry seasoning and chopped nuts in bowl. Dip roll in melted butter (1/2 Cup) then in crumbs.
6. Place on baking sheet and bake at 350° for 20 minutes.
7. Make gravy: Thicken broth that chicken was cooked in by stirring 1 tablespoon flour per cup of broth.
8. Cook, stirring constantly until thickened.
9. Stir in 1 envelope cream of Chicken Cup O Soup.
10. Remove rolls, let cool, cover in gravy, serve.

Yesterday is a canceled check, tomorrow is a promissory note, today is the only cash you have. Spend it wisely.
- Anonymous

Every morning you are handed 24 golden hours. They are one of the few things in this would that you get free of charge. If you had all the money in the world, you couldn't buy an extra hour. What will you do with this priceless treasure?
- Anonymous

Don't be fooled by the calendar. There are only as many days in the year as you make use of. One man gets only a week's value out of a year while another man gets a full year's value out of a week.
- Charles Richards

Oriental Chicken

Prep time: 30 minutes

    3 pounds chicken thighs or drummettes or wings
1 clove garlic
1/2 ginger
1 green onion
8-10 ounces Japanese style soy salad dressing
Cooking oil
1/2 cup water

1. Wash and pat dry chicken parts. Slice garlic and ginger.
2. In frying pan, fry chicken parts until oil comes out from chicken, then add garlic and ginger. Add green onion and continue frying until brown.
3. Add salad dressing and 1/2 cup water, cover and simmer for 10 minutes.

Microwave Baked Fish

Prep time: 25 minutes

1/2 cup chopped celery
1/2 cup chopped carrots
1/2 cup chopped onion
1 tablespoon olive oil
1 pound Cod or halibut or other farm fish
1/2 cup grated Swiss cheese
1/2 cup sliced mushrooms
1 to 2 tomatoes, chopped
3 tablespoons sherry

1. Sauté celery, carrots and onion in olive oil. When lightly browned, pour into buttered baking dish.
2. Arrange fish on bed of sautéed vegetables. Microwave on Bake at 60% for 5 minutes.
3. Meanwhile, sauté mushrooms in 1 tablespoon of butter, add sherry, then place on top of fish.
4. Add cheese and tomatoes. Microwave 2 more minutes. Serve and enjoy.

All time management begins with planning.
- Tom Greening

The whole point of getting things done is knowing what to leave undone.
- Lady Stella

Less is more.
- Mies van der Rohe

Chicken Salad Pitas

Prep time: 30 minutes

1-1/2 cups cubed cooked chicken
1 medium carrot, julienned
1/2 cup julienned cucumber
1/4 cup sliced radishes
1/4 cup sliced ripe olives
1/4 cup cubed mozzarella cheese
1/3 to 1/2 cup Italian salad dressing
5 pita breads (6-inch) halved
Lettuce leaves

1. In a bowl, combine the chicken, carrot, cucumber, radishes, olives and cheese.
2. Add dressing and toss to coat.
3. Line pita breads with lettuce leaves.
4. Stuff about 1/3 cup of chicken mixture into each half.

For fast acting relief; try slowing down.
- Lily Tomlin

More tips for a simpler life

Think about your values and write down those that really matter to you. What is most important? Spending time with family? Accumulating great wealth? Achieving powerful influence? Acquiring possessions? Expressing yourself? Learning new ideas? Experiencing adventure and travel? Maintaining excellent health? Socializing with friends? Contributing to the community? You can't do them all. Cut out activities that aren't consistent with your core values.

Write a list of goals you'd like to achieve. Focus on doing a few really well, rather than a lot in a mediocre way. You can't add hours to the day, but you can cut down on activities.

Give away clerical tasks to others who can handle non-priority activities.

Stop spending time to save money. Instead, spend money to save time. Don't drive across town to save a few cents on a grocery item. It's not worth your time. Do hire someone to do chores you're not fond of.

Cancel subscriptions to magazines you never get around to reading.

Only read one newspaper a day.

Cut back on television time. Only watch those shows you decide on beforehand. Circle them in the television-listing magazine. Then turn off the television when the program is over, or go for broke and give up watching television altogether.

Clean out your basement or your office. If you're not using something, get rid of it. Put an expiration date on items when you can't decide whether to keep them or not. Get rid of them when the expiration date arrives.

Quit organizations or groups that aren't contributing to your advancement, your network, or your fun.

Make a plan for the weekend that doesn't involve work. Plan to spend more time with your family or with people who make positive contributions to your life. Stop spending time with people who are a drain on your energy or vitality.

Carry a smaller wallet or purse. Start by cleaning out the one you've got. Get rid of unnecessary credit cards and other clutter that you don't use regularly.

Stop checking up on your financial portfolio every day. Most people invest for the long term. Checking your results daily adds to stress and might lead to expensive and unnecessary changes.

Cut back on debt. Consolidate your different debts into one and pay it off. Put your credit cards in a spot where you won't be able to use them until you're debt-free. Track your expenses for a month, then cut back your spending on items you don't need. For instance, pack a lunch rather than buying one at work. Mix and match your outfits rather than constantly buying new ones.

Cut back on your children's planned activities. If they have to use a time planner to schedule their activities, and you spend all of your time taxiing them around, they're probably too busy.

Five Cup Salad

Prep time: 30 minutes
Chill time: 3 hours

    1 cup miniature marshmallows
    1 cup mandarin oranges, drained
    1 cup pineapple tidbits, drained
    1 cup sour cream
    1 cup coconut

Mix all together. Refrigerate 3 hours.

Don't underestimate the value of doing nothing, of just going along, listening to all the things you can't hear, and not bothering.
                - Pooh's Little Instruction Book

Slow down and everything you are chasing will come around and catch you.
                - John De Paola

Asian Chicken Salad

Prep time: 25 minutes

2 cups cooked chicken
1 small head cabbage, diced
1 package Ramen Noodles, raw and smashed up
1/2 cup oil
2 tablespoons vinegar
Salt and pepper to taste

1. Boil chicken, let cook and break into small pieces.
2. Mix chicken cabbage and smashed Ramen Noodles together.
3. Combine package of noodle seasoning oil, vinegar and salt and pepper and mix to make dressing.
4. Pour dressing over chicken mixture and marinate over night.
5. Optional: before serving toast 1/2 cup almonds and 2 tablespoons sesame seeds in 350° F oven for 5 minutes or until golden and add just before you serve.

Danish Salad

Prep time: 25 minutes

    1 package Danish Dessert (Strawberry)
    1 large can chunk pineapple
    Strawberries (whole)
    Bananas (cut size of berries)
    Lemon Juice

1. Drain juice from pineapple. Add enough water to make 2 cups when combined. Heat while mixing according to pudding directions on package. Cook until thick.
2. Add fruit, chill, and serve.

Nature does not hurry, yet everything is accomplished.
- Lao Tzu

It's never to late – in fiction or in life – to revise.
- Nancy Thayer

Middle Eastern Spinach Salad

Prep time: 30 minutes

6 cups spinach leaves
1-1/4 cups chopped red apple
1/4 cup raisins
2 tablespoons chopped green onion
3 tablespoons vegetable oil
2 tablespoons cider vinegar
2 teaspoons apple curry chutney
3/4 teaspoon curry powder
1/2 teaspoon dry mustard
1/4 teaspoon salt

1. Combine spinach, chopped apples, raisins, and chopped green onion in large bowl; refrigerate for 10 minutes.
2. Combine vegetable oil, vinegar, chutney, curry powder, mustard, and salt in small bowl.
3. Pour over salad; toss well to coat.

Summer Vegetable Medley

Prep time: 30 minutes

1/2 cup butter or margarine, melted
1-1/4 teaspoons each minced fresh parsley, basil and chives
3/4 teaspoon salt
1/4 teaspoon pepper
3 medium ears sweet corn, husks removed, cut into 2-inch pieces
1 medium sweet red pepper, cut into 1-inch pieces
1 medium sweet yellow pepper cut into 1-inch pieces
1 medium zucchini, cut into 1/4-inch slices
10 large fresh mushrooms

1. In a large bowl, combine the butter, parsley, basil, chives, salt and pepper.
2. Add the vegetables, toss to coat.
3. Place vegetables in a disposable foil pan. Grill, covered, over medium-high heat for 5 minutes, stir.
4. Grill 5 minutes longer or until the vegetables are tender.

Basil Tomato Soup

Prep time: 30 minutes

2 cans (28-ounce) crushed tomatoes
1 can (14-ounce) chicken broth
18 to 20 fresh basil leaves, minced
1 teaspoon sugar
1 cup whipping cream
1/2 cup butter or margarine

1. In a large saucepan, bring the tomatoes and broth to a boil. Reduce heat, cover and simmer for 10 minutes.
2. Add basil and sugar. Reduce heat to low.
3. Stir in cream and butter. Cook until butter is melted.

Your house is your home only when you feel you have jurisdiction over it.
        - Joan Kron

The problem with property is that it takes so much of your time.
        - Willem de Kooning

More tips for simplifying your life

If you need to buy a specific item, call the stores to see if they have it in stock. If they do, ask them to set it aside for you. This saves an amazing amount of time running around looking for an item.

Don't procrastinate. It takes more time trying to figure out how to put off doing something then actually doing it. Save yourself the time and just tackle the job and get it over with.

When you run errands, plan to limit your trips to once or twice a week. Group tasks by geographic locations.

Put the videos that need to be returned in front of the door so you don't rush out leaving them behind.

Always do some kind of work when talking on the phone: Clean out your purse, unload the dishwasher, clean your shoes, sew a hem or button, do your nails, wash dishes, start dinner or set the table. The list of mindless tasks you can do while talking on the phone is endless and your mind is still with your conversation.

Don't play telephone tag: When you leave a message for someone, leave a detailed one so they don't have to call you back.

Don't clean up your child's room; teach him to do it himself. It will be better for both of you in the long run.

Choose one day, over the weekend when you have some time to cook and cook meals for the week. Even one or two meals will help a lot during the busy weekdays.

Let the answering machine pick up your calls for an afternoon. You can listen in on the messages so you can pick up anything that is an emergency. This will allow you to return calls at a more convenient time for you.

Have specific times during the day to read and answer your e-mail.

Live closer to your work so you don't have to drive.

Learn to set priorities on things like goals, tasks, meeting agenda items, interruptions etc. Start with "A-priority" tasks and make sure that they are the best use of your time.

Peach Dump Cake

Prep time: 10 minutes
Cook time: 45 minutes

    1 can peach pie filling
    1 small can (about 4-ounce) crushed pineapple
    1 box yellow cake mix
    1 cup butter, melted

1. In a 9x13 casserole dish, layer ingredients beginning with pie filling, then pineapple, then cake mix.
2. Pour melted butter over the top and bake at 350° F for 35-45 minutes or until top browns.

Precisely the least, the softest, lightest, a lizard's rustling, a breath, a flash, a moment – a little makes the way of the best happiness
        - Frederich Nietzxche

Cinnamon Pull-Apart Rolls

1/2 cup sugar
2-1/2 teaspoons cinnamon
1/3 cup butter, melted
1 can (12-ounce) refrigerated buttermilk
   flaky biscuits

1. Preheat oven to 400° F.
2. Generously grease an 8x4 loaf pan with solid shortening, not butter.
3. In small bowl combine sugar and cinnamon and mix well.
4. Separate dough into 10 biscuits and cut each biscuit into 4 pieces.
5. Dip each piece in melted butter and roll in cinnamon sugar mixture.
6. Place coated dough pieces in greased loaf pan
7. Bake at 400° F for 20-25 minutes until bread is golden brown.
8. Cool for 2 minutes, then loosen edges of bread and remove from pan.

Mile High Strawberry Pie

Prep time: 10 minutes

2 egg whites
1 cup sugar or substitute
1/4 teaspoon cream of tarter
1-1/4 cup sliced strawberries

1. Combine above ingredients in mixer and mix for 7 minutes on high.
2. Add 1 to 2 cups cool whip.
3. Pile high into a graham cracker ready make crust and freeze.
4. Eat right out of freezer.

There must be quite a few things that a hot bath won't cure, but I don't know many of them.
- Sylvia Plath

You can eat an elephant if you do it one bite at a time.
- Robert Riley

Brownie Pie

1 9-inch piecrust
1 cup chocolate chips
1 (15-ounce) package brownie mix
1/3 cup water
1 egg
1 square semisweet chocolate, melted

1. Sprinkle chocolate chips over the bottom of crust lined pan.
2. Beat together brownie mix, water, egg, and melted chocolate in a medium bowl.
3. Pour over chips in pie pan.
4. Bake at 375° F for 35-40 minutes until crust is golden brown and brownie top is shiny and appears done.

The time to relax is when you don't have time for it.
- Attributed to both Jim Goodwin
and Sydney J. Harris

Microwave Fudge

Prep time: 25 minutes

> 1/2 cup butter
> 3-1/2 cups powdered sugar
> 1/2 cup cocoa
> 1/4 cup milk
> 1 teaspoon vanilla
> 1/2 cup chopped nuts

1. Place ingredients (except nuts) in bowl. Do not mix.
2. Microwave on high power for two minutes.
3. Beat with electric mixer until smooth.
4. Fold in nuts.
5. Pour mixture into buttered 8x8 dish.
6. Refrigerate 15 to 20 minutes until set.

We struggle with the complexities and avoid the simplicities.

- Norman Vincent Peale

Honeydew Wedges

Prep time: 15 minutes
Chilling time: 3 hours

1 honeydew melon
1 3-ounce package lemon flavor gelatin
1/2 cup boiling water
1/2 cup ice water
Ice cubes
1 cup whole strawberries

1. Cut melon in half and scoop out seeds. Pat the inside of the melon dry using paper towels and set aside.
2. Dissolve gelatin in boiling water. Stir until no sugar particles are visible. Combine ice water and ice cubes to make one cup. Add to gelatin and stir until slightly thickened. Remove any unmelted ice.
3. Place each melon half in a small bowl to hold straight and firm. Place half of strawberries in each melon half.
4. Pour gelatin mixture over berries. Cover with plastic wrap and chill until firm, about 3 hours. Serve!

Fruit Tacos

Prep time: 15 minutes

  5 cups assorted chopped or sliced fresh fruit
  12 hard taco shells
  2 tablespoons orange juice
  8 ounces low fat strawberry yogurt
  1/2 cup toasted coconut
  1/2 cup sliced almonds

1. Combine fruit and orange juice in large bowl.
2. Fill taco shells with fruit mixture. Top with yogurt, coconut and almonds.

Live simply, so others may simply live.
- Gandhi

Reduce the complexity of life by eliminating the needless want of life, and the labors of life reduce themselves.
- Edwin Teale

Butterscotch Haystacks

Prep time: 10 minutes

1-2/3 cups butterscotch flavored morsels
3/4 cup creamy peanut butter
8-1/2 ounces chow mein noodles
7 ounces miniature marshmallows

1. Line cookie sheet with waxed paper.
2. Microwave chips in large, microwave-safe bowl on medium-high for 1 minute; stir. Microwave an additional 10 to 20 second intervals, stirring until smooth.
3. Stir in peanut butter until well blended. Add chow mein noodles and marshmallows; toss until all ingredients are coated. Drop by rounded tablespoon onto prepared trays.
4. Refrigerate until ready to serve.

Nature uses as little as possible of anything.
- Johannes Keppler

Apple Crisp

Prep time: 15 minutes
Cooking time: 45 minutes

    7 or 8 apples
    1 cup sugar, brown or white
    Juice of 1 lemon
    1 cup flour
    1/2 cup butter

1. Peel and slice apples and place in baking pan.
2. Sprinkle 1/2 cup sugar and lemon juice over apples.
3. Beat flour, butter and remaining sugar together and then crumble over apples.
4. Bake at 350° F for 45 minutes.

To find the universal elements enough; to find the air and the water exhilarating; to be refreshed by a morning walk or an evening saunter... to be thrilled by the stars at night; to be elated over a bird's nest or a wildflower in spring – these are some of the rewards of the simple life.
                                    - John Burroughs

If you have to pack a lunch & you're tired of Peanut butter and Jelly...

These lunch box recipes are perfect for everyone. It doesn't matter if you're a college student and you're on campus all day; a mom trying to think of something different for your kids to take to school, or you just want to brown bag it for work. You'll never get bored with lunch when you use these easy and great tasting recipes.

Spicy Egg Salad Sandwiches

Prep time: 25 minutes

1 (4-ounce) can diced green chilies
4 hard cooked eggs
3 tablespoons light mayonnaise dressing or fat-free
    mayonnaise dressing
2 tablespoons sliced green onion
1/4 teaspoon hot pepper sauce
4 bagels or English muffins

1. Combine chilies, eggs, mayonnaise dressing, green onion and hot pepper sauce in medium bowl. Season with salt and ground black pepper.
2. Spread egg salad on toasted bagels or English muffins.

Things should be as simple as possible, but not simpler.
- Albert Einstein

Pop Corn Balls

Prep time: 20 minutes

   1/3 cup white corn syrup
   1/3 cup water
   3/4 teaspoon vanilla
   3 quarts popcorn
   3/4 teaspoon salt
   1/4 cup butter
   1 cup sugar

1. Pop popcorn.
2. Combine all ingredients except vanilla.
3. Cook to 270° F or until mixture forms a brittle ball in cold water.
4. Remove from stove, and add vanilla and then combine with popped corn.

Simplicity is the essence of happiness.
- Cedric Bledsoe

Tortilla Roll-ups

Prep time: 10 minutes

   Flour tortilla
   1 slice of ham
   1 slice of cheese

1. Place ham and cheese on tortilla in microwave on high for 45 seconds, to almost melt cheese.
2. Close up one end of the tortilla by folding it in a little, and roll tortilla up like a small burrito.
3. Wrap rolled tortilla in paper towel, then aluminum foil to keep the moisture down and the heat in.

If your mind isn't clouded by unnecessary things, this is the best season of your life.
- Wu-Men

Pita Sandwiches

Prep time: 10 minutes

Pita bread half
Leaf of lettuce
Tomato
Ham or turkey
Cheese
Ranch salad dressing or mayo, mustard or
favorite condiment

1. Gently open pita, pour small amount of dressing in, spreading on both sides of pita.
2. Place in lettuce leaf, tomato, meat and cheese in stacked layers.

Voluntary simplicity means going fewer places in one day rather than more, seeing less so I can see more, doing less so I can do more, acquiring less so I can have more.
- John Kabat-Zinn

Crescent Sandwiches

Prep time: 20 minutes

    1 can refrigerated crescent roll dough
    Ham or turkey
    Cheese

1. Place 1 slice of meat and 1 slice of cheese in crescent roll before rolling into shape.
2. Roll up and bake according to directions on can.

Practically speaking, a life that is vowed to simplicity, appropriate boldness, good humor, gratitude, unstinting work and play, and lots of walking brings us close to the actual existing world and its wholeness.
- Gary Snyder

96

Triscuit Nachos

Prep time: 10 minutes

Triscuit Crackers
Salsa
Cheese

1. Place crackers on a microwave-safe plate.
2. Cover with salsa, top with cheese.
3. Melt and let cool, place in small plastic container.

That man is richest whose pleasures are the cheapest.
- Henry David Thoreau

The ability to simplify means to eliminate the
unnecessary so that the necessary may speak.
- Hans Hofmann

Waffle Sandwich

Prep time: 5 minutes

   2 frozen waffles
   Almond butter
   Sliced banana

1. Toast waffles.
2. Spread almond butter on one waffle and place sliced banana on top of that.
3. Place the other waffle on top.

Man is an over-complicated organism. If he is doomed to extinction he will die out for want of simplicity.
- Ezra Pound

Pasta Salad

Prep time: 20 minutes

Curly pasta, prepared as directed
Ricotta cheese
Sliced spinach leaves

1. Drain pasta and toss together with ricotta cheese (three heaping tablespoons per cup of cooked pasta) and strips of sliced spinach leaves.
2. Pack in sealable containers.

Veggie Dipping Sauce

Prep time: 3 minutes

1/4 of a shredded cucumber
Single serving plain yogurt

Mix ingredients together and pack the dip in a sealable plastic container.

Peanut-butter Extravaganza

Ingredients
Sandwich bread
Peanut butter
Bananas
Marshmallows
Jam

1. Spread a slice of bread with peanut butter.
2. Slice up a banana and place it on the left third.
3. Add marshmallows beside the bananas on the center third.
4. Spread jam over the remaining third and top with a second slice of bread.

In the hope of reaching the moon men fail to see the flowers that blossom at their feet.
- Albert Schweitzer

Simple pleasures are the last refuge of the complex.
- Oscar Wilde

Cutting your Grocery Bills

Cutting your grocery bills doesn't necessarily save you time, but then again, time is money, so take a day off work, after all, you'll save the money you would have made by trying some of these money saving tips next time you stop by the grocery store.

Be aware of the techniques stores use to get you to buy. Necessities such as milk are usually at the back of the store to get you to walk by all the other aisles first. Profitable items are usually at your eye level. The bakery is usually at the front of the store to entice you to buy with the fresh baked smell. Items at the end of an aisle doesn't necessarily mean a lower price.

Always check your receipt before you leave the store. The computerized scanners may have been input with the wrong or non-sale price. Cashiers can make mistakes so keep your eyes open.

Plan ahead by listing the items you need. Try not to shop more than once a week. The more you go, the more you'll be tempted to pick up something you don't need. It also wastes time since you'll have to drive to the store again and wait at the check-out line.

Try to stick to your shopping list when you're in the store, but be flexible if you find a good bargain.

Before deciding n a store, compare the advertised specials and what you need. Most stores will have loss leaders to lure you in, but other items you need may cost you more.

Stock up on items that will keep and that you can use if you can get a bulk discount.

Store brands or generic items are always cheaper.

Convenience foods usually cost more and give you less. Make your own TV dinner by freezing your leftovers. Buy prepared foods only if the time you save is more valuable than the price you pay.

Cut your own meats. It's generally cheaper to buy a whole chicken than one that has been cut up for you. Cut your own beef into cubes for stew.

Shop during off peak hours and after you've eaten. If you're hungry, you'll be in a hurry and less likely to compare prices. If the store is busy and you're waiting in line, you'll have more opportunities to buy expensive impulsive items close to the check-out.

Don't forget to use coupons. If you find more coupons at the store but don't need the items, save the coupons for future use.

So easy kids can make them, and you can too!

Sometimes young children want to help in the kitchen so I added some great recipes that they will enjoy helping you prepare. If you are a kid or just feel like one, these recipes take next to no time to make and taste great! Who knows, making them may even be more fun than eating them.

Bumps on a Log

Prep time: 5 minutes

    1 celery stalk, washed, ends trimmed
    2 tablespoons creamy or chunky peanut butter
    10 Nestle Raisinets milk chocolate covered raisins

1. Fill celery with peanut butter.
2. Press raisinets into peanut butter.

Berry Delight

Prep time: 10 minutes

    1 bag frozen mixed berries
    1 pkg. individual sponge cakes, piecrust, or pastries
    1-2 cups sugar (to taste)
    1 container whipped topping

1. Thaw berries, add sugar to taste.
2. Spoon berries over cakes, crusts or pastries.
3. Top with topping, serve.

Twinkie Cake

Prep time: 15 minutes

    1 box of Twinkie Cakes
    1 carton frozen strawberries-with syrup (thawed)
    1 tub cool-whip (thawed)

1. Slice Twinkies in half, laying bottom half filling side up in the bottom of a cake pan, covering the entire bottom of the pan.
2. Pour strawberries over bottom layer and place the topside of the Twinkies over berries.
3. Frost the cake with cool-whip and serve.

My riches consist not in the extent of my possessions but in the fewness of my wants.
                - J. Botherton

The day is of infinite length for him who knows how to appreciate and use it.
                - Goethe

Plurality should not be assumed without necessity.
                - William of Ockham

Fruit Kabobs

Prep time: 5 minutes

Toothpicks or wooden skewers
2 or 3 pieces of fruit per skewer (try melon balls,
    grapes, bananas or strawberries)
A handful of miniature marshmallows
3/4 cup plain yogurt
2 tablespoons real maple syrup

1. Alternate fruit, cheese, and marshmallows on stick.
2. Make dipping sauce: combine yogurt and maple syrup in bowl and whisk together.
3. Dip kabobs in sauce.

It is the sweet, simple things of life which are the real ones after all.
                        - Laura Ingalls Wilder

Be wary of any enterprise that requires new clothes.
                        - Henry David Thoreau

Crispy Pops

Prep time: 15 minutes
Cool time 30 minutes

1/4 cup margarine
1 (10-ounce) package miniature marshmallows
6 cups of crisped rice cereal
1 cup M&M's candy
12 (5-ounce) size paper cups (wax lined works best)
12 Popsicle sticks

1. Combine cereal and M&M's, set aside.
2. In a large saucepan over medium heat, melt margarine and marshmallows together, stirring constantly.
3. Combine marshmallow mixture with cereal mixture and stir well.
4. Mix completely until all cereal is coated.
5. Spoon mixture into paper cups and press lightly to fill.
6. Insert Popsicle sticks into the center of the mixture and press again lightly with fingers. Cool.
7. If you like, press half of the mixture into a 9x9 square baking pan and cool, Cut into squares.

Handy Cooking Tips

Stuff a miniature marshmallow in the bottom of a sugar cone to prevent ice cream drips.

To keep potatoes from budding, place an apple in the bag with the potatoes.

To prevent eggshells from cracking, add a pinch of salt to the water before hard boiling.

Run your hands under cold water before pressing Rice Krispies treats in the pan, the marshmallow won't stick to your fingers.

To get the most juice out of fresh lemons, bring them to room temperature and roll them under your palm against the kitchen counter before squeezing.

To easily remove burnt-on food from your skillet, add a drop or two of dish soap and enough water to cover the bottom of the pan and bring it to a boil. The skillet will be much easier to clean.

Spray your Tupperware with nonstick cooking spray before pouring in tomato-base sauces, no more stains!

When a cake recipe calls for flouring the baking pan, use a bit of the dry cake mix instead, no white mess on the outside of the cake.

If you accidentally over-salt a dish while it's still cooking, drop in a peeled potato, it absorbs the excess salt for an instant fix me up.

Wrap celery in aluminum foil when putting on the refrigerator, it will keep for weeks.

When boiling corn on the cob, add a pinch of sugar to help bring out the corn's natural sweetness.

To determine whether an egg is fresh, immerse it in a pan of cool, salted water. If it sinks, it is fresh, if it rises to the surface, throw it away.

Potatoes will take food stains off your fingers. Just slice and rub raw potato on the stains and rinse with water.

Order these additional Cookbooks from The American Pantry Collection

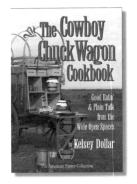
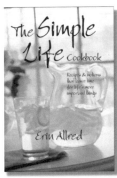

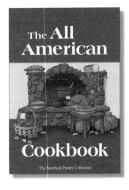

Order Online! www.apricotpress.com

Apricot Press Order Form

Book Title	Quantity	x	Cost / Book	=	Total

All Cook Books are $9.95 US.

Do not send Cash. Mail check or money order to:
**Apricot Press   P.O. Box 98
Nephi, Utah   84648**
Telephone 435-623-1929
Allow 3 weeks for delivery.

**Quantity discounts available.
Call us for more information.**
9 a.m. - 5 p.m. MST

Sub Total =

Shipping = $2.00

Tax 8.5% =

Total Amount Enclosed =

Shipping Address

Name:

Street:

City: State:

Zip Code:

Telephone:

Email: